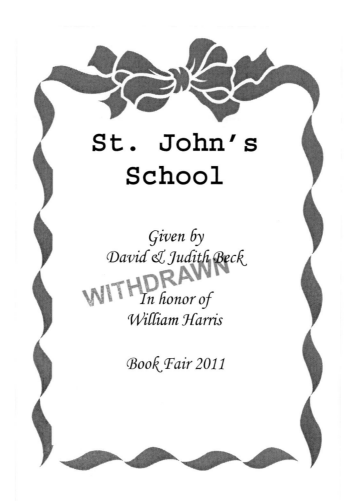

St. John's
School

Given by
David & Judith Beck

WITHDRAWN

In honor of
William Harris

Book Fair 2011

Pebble® Plus

Science Builders

Learning about Rocks

by Mari Schuh

Consulting Editor: Gail Saunders-Smith, PhD

Consultant: Joanne K. Olson, PhD
Associate Professor, Science Education
Center for Excellence in Science & Mathematics Education
Iowa State University, Ames

CAPSTONE PRESS
a capstone imprint

Pebble Plus is published by Capstone Press,
151 Good Counsel Drive, P.O. Box 669, Mankato, Minnesota 56002.
www.capstonepub.com

Books published by Capstone Press are manufactured with paper
containing at least 10 percent post-consumer waste.

Library of Congress Cataloging-in-Publication Data
Schuh, Mari C., 1975–
  Learning about rocks / by Mari Schuh.
     p. cm.—(Pebble Plus. Science builders)
  Includes bibliographical references and index.
  Summary: "Simple text and full-color photographs provides a brief introduction to rocks and how they form"—Provided
by publisher.
  ISBN 978-1-4296-6072-3 (library binding)
  ISBN 978-1-4296-7108-8 (paperback)
  1. Mineralogy—Juvenile literature. 2. Rocks—Juvenile literature. 3. Minerals—Juvenile literature. I. Title. II. Series.
  QE365.2.S38 2012
  552—dc22   2010053933

Editorial Credits
Erika L. Shores, editor; Bobbie Nuytten, designer; Wanda Winch, media researcher; Laura Manthe, production specialist

Photo Credits
iStockphoto Inc.: dominiquelandau, 11 (top right), Nancy Nehring, 13 (left), Phil Augustavo, 13 (right), Stephen Morris, 15
(left); Photodisc, 9; Shutterstock: Anatoli Styf, cover, 1, Bork, 19, Cecilia Lim H M, 21, Douglas Adams, 7, Jan Kranendonk,
5, Michal Baranski, 11 (bottom), Ng Yin Chern, 17, Oksana Perkins, 15 (right), TTphoto, 22-23, 24, Tyler Boyes, 11
(top left)

Note to Parents and Teachers

The Science Builders series supports national science standards related to earth science. This
book describes and illustrates rocks. The images support early readers in understanding the
text. The repetition of words and phrases helps early readers learn new words. This book
also introduces early readers to subject-specific vocabulary words, which are defined in the
Glossary section. Early readers may need assistance to read some words and to use the Table of
Contents, Glossary, Read More, Internet Sites, and Index sections of the book.

Printed in the United States of America in North Mankato, Minnesota.
032011   006110CGF11

Table of Contents

What Are Rocks?

Tiny rocks line beaches.

Tall mountains reach high in the sky.

Rocks are almost everywhere.

Where can you find rocks?

Rocks are solid minerals.

A mineral is something found

in nature that isn't made by

people, plants, or animals.

Earth is a rocky planet.

The crust is solid rock.

Below the crust is molten rock

called the mantle. Earth's core

is molten and solid.

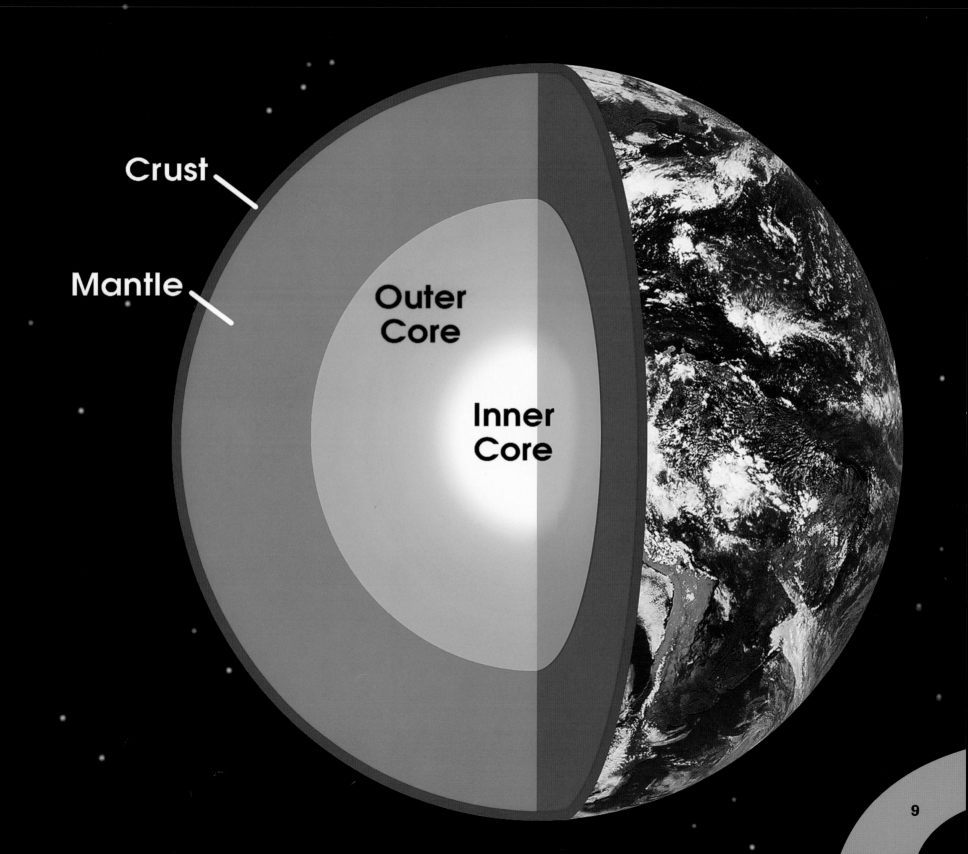

Crust

Mantle

Outer Core

Inner Core

Kinds of Rocks

Three main kinds of rocks
are found on Earth.
Igneous, sedimentary,
and metamorphic rocks form
in different ways.

igneous

sedimentary

metamorphic

11

Granite is a kind of igneous rock formed when magma cools underground. Obsidian is an igneous rock formed when magma cools above ground.

granite

obsidian

Layers of tiny rocks, sand, and mud build up over time. Pressure hardens this sediment into rock. Sedimentary rocks like shale and sandstone form.

shale

sandstone

Fossils are found in sedimentary rock.

Fossils are the remains of plants

and animals that were buried

in sediment.

Metamorphic rocks are made from other rocks. Heat and pressure deep inside Earth can change rocks from one kind to another. Marble is a metamorphic rock.

marble

Always Changing

Wind, water, heat, and pressure slowly break down rocks. Rocks are always changing. In the future, the rocks around you could look different.

Glossary

crust—the outer layer of Earth

igneous rock—rock that forms when magma cools

magma—melted rock found under the earth's surface

mantle—the layer of molten rock below Earth's crust

metamorphic rock—rock that is changed by heat and pressure

mineral—a solid substance found in nature that is not made by people, animals, or plants

molten—melted by heat

pressure—the force produced by pressing on something

sediment—bits of rocks, sand, and mud that are carried to a place by water or wind

sedimentary rock—rock formed by layers of rocks, sand, or mud that have been pressed together

Read More

Mayer, Cassie. *Rock.* Materials. Chicago: Heinemann Library, 2008.

Petersen, Christine. *Rockin' Rocks.* Rock On! Edina, Minn.: ABDO Pub. Co., 2010.

Pitts, Zachary. *The Pebble First Guide to Rocks and Minerals.* Mankato, Minn.: Capstone Press, 2009.

Internet Sites

FactHound offers a safe, fun way to find Internet sites related to this book. All of the sites on FactHound have been researched by our staff.

Here's all you do:

Visit *www.facthound.com*

Type in this code: 9781429660723

Check out projects, games and lots more at
www.capstonekids.com

Index

Word Count: 197
Grade: 1
Early-Intervention Level: 24